Must See Places Of The World

Speedy Publishing LLC
40 E. Main St. #1156
Newark, DE 19711

www.speedypublishing.com

Copyright 2014
9781635013351
First Printed November 24, 2014

 speedypublishing

Zimbabwe

Victoria Falls, or Mosi-oa-Tunya (Tokaleya Tonga: the Smoke that Thunders), is a waterfall in southern Africa on the Zambezi River at the border of Zambia and Zimbabwe. David Livingstone, the Scottish missionary and explorer, is believed to have been the first European to view Victoria Falls on 16 November 1855 from what is now known as Livingstone Island

Moscow, Russia

Saint Basil's Cathedral, is a church in Red Square in Moscow, Russia. The building, now a museum, is officially known as the Cathedral of the Intercession of the Most Holy Theotokos on the Moat or Pokrovsky Cathedral. A world famous landmark, it has been the hub of the city's growth since the 14th century and was the city's tallest building until the completion of the Ivan the Great Bell Tower in 1600.

New Zealand

Lake Taupo is a lake situated in the North Island of New Zealand. Otumuheke Stream (hot river) winds its way through a series of small natural hot pools, merging with the mighty Waikato River at Spa Park to create a wonderful free swimming hole. It is a great place to relax and soak in the open air.

Bali, Indonesia

Bali is an island and province of Indonesia. Bali is the largest tourist destination in the country and is renowned for its highly developed arts, including traditional and modern dance, sculpture, painting, leather, metalworking, and music. Since the late 20th century, the province has had a rise in tourism.

Iceland Waterfalls

Iceland Waterfalls are perhaps the country's most recognizable series of attractions. They're everywhere! Its collection of waterfalls rivals any other country in sheer power and raw beauty. The falls range from powerful and wide river-type monsters like Dettifoss, Gullfoss, and Goðafoss to tall and narrow ones like Glymur, Háifoss, and Hengifoss.

Berlin, Germany

Berlin is the capital of Germany and one of the 16 states of Germany. Berlin is one of the few cities that has three UNESCO World Heritage sites. The famous Museum Island and the Prussian castles and gardens were joined in 2008 by the Berlin modernist housing estates. In 2006 the German capital was awarded the title "UNESCO City of Design".

Dubai

The Palm Islands are two artificial islands, Palm Jumeirah and Palm Jebel Ali, on the coast of Dubai, United Arab Emirates. This island takes the form of a palm tree, topped by a crescent.

Paris

The Eiffel Tower (French: La tour Eiffel, is an iron lattice tower located on the Champ de Mars in Paris. It was named after the engineer Gustave Eiffel, whose company designed and built the tower. Millions of people climb the Eiffel Tower every year and it has had over 250 million visitors since its opening.

Cambodia

Angkor Wat was first a Hindu, later a Buddhist, temple complex in Cambodia and the largest religious monument in the world. The temple is at the top of the high classical style of Khmer architecture. It has become a symbol of Cambodia, appearing on its national flag, and it is the country's prime attraction for visitors.

Pisa, Italy

The Leaning Tower of Pisa (Italian: Torre pendente di Pisa) or simply the Tower of Pisa (Torre di Pisa) is the campanile, or freestanding bell tower, of the cathedral of the Italian city of Pisa, known worldwide for its unintended tilt to one side.

Turkey

The Temple of Artemis or Artemision, also known less precisely as the Temple of Diana, was a Greek temple dedicated to the goddess Artemis and is one of the Seven Wonders of the Ancient World.

Wiltshire, England

Stonehenge is a prehistoric monument located in Wiltshire, England, about 2 miles (3 km) west of Amesbury and 8 miles (13 km) north of Salisbury. One of the most famous sites in the world, Stonehenge is the remains of a ring of standing stones set within earthworks.

Venice, Italy

Grand Canal, Italian Canale Grande, main waterway of Venice, Italy, following a natural channel that traces a reverse-S course from San Marco Basilica to Santa Chiara Church and divides the city into two parts. The Grand Canal is approximately 2.5 miles long and averages at a depth of about 16 feet. Over 15 million tourists visit Venice each year.

Tinum, Mexico

Chichen Itza, was a large pre-Columbian city built by the Maya people of the Terminal Classic. The archaeological site is located in the municipality of Tinum, in the Mexican state of Yucatán. Chichen Itza is one of the most visited archaeological sites in Mexico; an estimated 1.2 million tourists visit the ruins every year.

Vatican City

St. Peter's Basilica is a Late Renaissance church located within Vatican City. St. Peter's is the most renowned work of Renaissance architecture and remains one of the largest churches in the world.

London

Big Ben is the nickname for the Great Bell of the clock at the north end of the Palace of Westminster in London, and often extended to refer to the clock and the clock tower. The tower holds the largest four-faced chiming clock in the world and is the third-tallest free-standing clock tower.

El Giza, Egypt

The Great Pyramid of Giza (also known as the Pyramid of Khufu or the Pyramid of Cheops) is the oldest and largest of the three pyramids in the Giza Necropolis bordering what is now El Giza, Egypt. It is the oldest of the Seven Wonders of the Ancient World, and the only one to remain largely intact.

Brazil

The exquisite Iguazu Falls are also known as the Iguassu Falls and the Iguaçu Falls. The magnificent spectacle of these 275 individual drops has awed tourists, locals and indigenous inhabitants for centuries. They originate from the Iguazu River and are located on the border of Brazil (in the state of Paraná) and Argentina.

China

The Great Wall of China is a series of fortifications made of stone, brick, tamped earth, wood, and other materials, generally built along an east-to-west line across the historical northern borders of China in part to protect the Chinese Empire or its prototypical states against intrusions by various nomadic groups or military incursions by various warlike peoples or forces.

Peru

Machu Picchu is a 15th-century Inca site located on a ridge between the Huayna Picchu and Machu Picchu mountains in Peru. The site's excellent preservation, the quality of its architecture, and the breathtaking mountain vista it occupies has made Machu Picchu one of the most famous archaeological sites in the world today.

Brazil

Rio de Janeiro is the capital city of the state of Rio de Janeiro and is second largest city in the South American country of Brazil. "Rio" as the city is commonly abbreviated is also the third largest metropolitan area in Brazil. It is considered one of the main tourist destinations in the Southern Hemisphere and is famous for its beaches, Carnaval celebration and various landmarks such as the statue of Christ the Redeemer.

Arizona, U.S.A

Grand Canyon National Park is the United States' 15th oldest national park. Named a UNESCO World Heritage Site in 1979, the park is located in Arizona. The park's central feature is the Grand Canyon, a gorge of the Colorado River, which is often considered one of the Seven Natural Wonders of the World. The park covers 1,217,262 acres (492,608 ha) of unincorporated area in Coconino and Mohave counties.

India

The Taj Mahal is a white marble mausoleum located in Agra, Uttar Pradesh, India. It was built by Mughal emperor Shah Jahan in memory of his third wife, Mumtaz Mahal. The Taj Mahal is widely recognized as "the jewel of Muslim art in India and one of the universally admired masterpieces of the world's heritage".

Made in the USA
Middletown, DE
28 November 2017